Gillingham
Shaftesbury
Marnhull
Fontmell Magna
Ashmore
Hammoon
Iwerne Minster
Farnham
Wimborne St Giles
Edmondsham
Tarrant Hinton
Gussage All Saints
Stourpaine
Long Crichel
Durweston
Tarrant Monkton
Horton
Witchampton
Hinton Martel
Blandford Forum
Stanbridge
Holt
Milton Abbas
Spetisbury
Shapwick
Pamphill
Bingham's Melcombe
Cowgrove
Wimborne
Winterborne Whitechurch
Almer
Winterborne Zelston
Throop
Holdenhurst
Tolpuddle
Wick
Mudeford
Poole
Bournemouth
Wareham
East Lulworth
Steeple
Blackmanston
Corfe Castle
West Lulworth
Tyneham
Kimmeridge
Kingston
Swanage
Lulworth Cove
Worth Matravers
St Alban's Head

the Villages of Dorset

OTHER FINE BOOKS ON DORSET FROM ENSIGN PUBLICATIONS

Dorset Murders — Roger Guttridge

Ten Dorset Mysteries — Roger Guttridge

Dorset Customs, Curiosities and Country Lore — Mary Brown

The Landscapes of Dorset — Roger Guttridge, Roger Holman and Roger Lane

The Echo Book of Heritage in Dorset and the New Forest — Roger Guttridge

Purbeck Shop : A Stoneworker's Story of Stone — Eric Benfield

Dorset Place-Names — David Mills

the Villages of Dorset

PHOTOGRAPHS BY

ROGER HOLMAN AND ROGER LANE

WORDS BY

ROGER GUTTRIDGE

First published in 1993 by
Ensign Publications
2 Redcar Street,
Southampton SO1 5LL.

Publisher David Graves.
Designed and typeset by Precinct Press.
Cover design by The Design Laboratory.
Endpapers designed by Sylvie Guttridge
Film reproduction by MRM Graphics, Winslow.
Printed in Europe.

ISBN 185455 095 0

CONTENTS

THE VILLAGES OF DORSET

ABOVE: **PAMPHILL**

FRONT COVER: **STOURPAINE**

INTRODUCTION

PHOTOGRAPHING THE VILLAGES OF DORSET

It is probably every town dweller's dream to shed the shackles of urban life and sample the peace and quiet of country living. Few things hold more appeal for the stress-ridden urbanite than the chance to exchange choking exhaust fumes for the sweet smell of freshly-mown hay and the drone of traffic noise for a musical backcloth of gentle birdsong.

At almost any time of the year there is a rustic "back to nature" feel about village life. The surrounding countryside probably has much to do with this. One has only to view a cluster of houses in the fold of a hill, protectively overlooked by a church spire or tower, to feel an immediate sense of homeliness and comfort. It was perhaps this "village in the landscape" image which first prompted the idea of photographing the villages of Dorset. They may not have quite the appeal of mellowed Cotswold stone or the half-timbered masterpieces of Shakespeare's Midlands but Dorset's villages do have a homely, lived-in quality wherein, perhaps, lies their true charm.

Photographing such tranquil scenes sounds at first like a relatively easy task. Even in the late 20th century, Dorset remains an essentially rural county, conjuring up images of pastoral countryside and attractive, rustic cottages sitting prettily around a village green and presided over by the parish church, the village inn and the general store or post office.

Unlike the artist, who can omit the occasional "For Sale" sign or the odd parked vehicle, the photographer has to accept the image presented to him. It was these elements of modern living — elements which we have all come to accept so readily — which became positive intrusions in our endeavours to photograph the timeless quality of each village.

There will always be some intrusions, of course. Motor cars, traffic signs, power and telephone lines, television aerials, satellite dishes and even plastic refuse sacks have forced their way into the village scene, in most cases never to be removed. Modern building materials can also exact a high price for their improved insulation and maintenance free qualities, for they generally lack the rustic charm of hand-hewn wood and cast iron. The changed face of the modern Dorset village has probably changed for good.

It is, however, the timeless quality that we have set out to capture, the delightful corners of rural Dorset which have weathered decades of change and which, we sense, will still be there, steadfast and solid, for many years to come. In selecting our viewpoints we have turned our backs, as far as possible, on the modern intrusions, focussing instead on the quieter corners of the village scene which, as yet, remain untarnished by modern living.

As in most counties, some villages have become tourist shrines. Corfe Castle and Abbotsbury are the obvious examples. Here tasteful preservation and strict planning controls have preserved a strong element of dignity even amid the throngs of summer visitors. Corfe and Abbotsbury inevitably offer much in the way of photographic charm, but away from the main roads and tourist routes lie scores of villages and hamlets which are known to most people only as names on a map or a signpost. Villages like Stoke Abbott, Netherbury and Little Bredy have retained a timeless charm, thanks largely to their relative seclusion. In such communities as these it is possible even today to experience a quality of life which many only dream of.

Meanwhile, let us not forget the villagers themselves, some of whom still live in cottages which their ancestors occupied before them. These are the people without whom there would be no Dorset villages — the families who, for generations, have influenced the shape and character of their rural communities. Many have proved resistant to change but that is to our advantage for it has ensured a reasonable balance between progress and preservation. These days the number of long-established inhabitants is diminishing. Those that remain now share their villages with ever-growing numbers of "incomers" — people who have retired to the country, commute from the country or spend their weekends there. Together, these people are the custodians of modern rural Dorset. To them falls the responsibility of preserving and enhancing the fabric of village life, as their predecessors have done for hundreds of years.

Photographing the villages of Dorset has been both fascinating and frustrating. But if through the medium of our photography we have captured those elements of the village scene that are worth retaining, then that task will also have been tremendously rewarding.

Roger Lane and Roger Holman
Wimborne, September 1993.

ABOVE: CHIDEOCK

In the sidestreets at Chideock, the cob and sandstone cottages enjoy a degree of tranquility not shared by their neighbours in the main street, where trunk route traffic bisects the village. North of the main road is the site of Chideock Castle, built in the 14th century and destroyed in the 17th by Civil War. Chideock is a very ancient village, referred to in the Domesday Book as "Chidihoc". But the locals have long since silenced the middle "i" or "e", preferring to pronounce it "Chiddick".

OPPOSITE: SEATOWN

Less than a mile south of Chideock is Seatown, the remnant of a once thriving fishing village forced into retreat by coastal erosion. In the 18th and 19th centuries it was also a great smuggling centre and in the 17th it provided a landing place for an advance party from the Duke of Monmouth's rebels. Seatown's shingle beach is overlooked from the west by Golden Cap, the highest cliff in southern England at 626 feet. It takes its name from its exposed crest of upper greensand, which glistens in the sunlight.

ABOVE: WEST BAY

West Bay was formerly called Bridport Harbour, a tiny port which grew up to serve the nearby town of Bridport and its famous rope industry, which has survived the ups and downs of centuries. The port dates back at least to medieval times, the man-made harbour to 1740. It became West Bay in 1884 when the Great Western Railway extended their line and wanted a name more in keeping with a holiday resort than a working port.

OPPOSITE: WEST BAY

West Bay's church was built as recently as 1936 but it has several buildings which are older and more interesting. These include a terrace of five unusually tall houses, built in 1885 by E. S. Prior (gable end in picture). They are reminiscent more of Normandy or Brittany than of a Dorset coastal village. In fact, their distinctly French appearance apparently led to the choice of West Bay as a training area for the Dieppe Raid in 1942.

ABOVE: BURTON BRADSTOCK

Burton Bradstock is one of many Dorset villages that save their best for those who trouble to leave their cars and look beyond the main road. It has a network of lanes, lined to a great extent by pretty thatched cottages, many dating from the 17th and 18th centuries and built in local stone. There are also some Georgian houses with stone walls at the back and sides and more expensive brick at the front. Burton Bradstock is quite a large village and is matched in scale by the church, which is mostly 15th century. Officially it is dedicated to St Mary but in John Hutchins' time it was St Lawrence whom the parishioners acknowledged.

ABOVE: BURTON BRADSTOCK

In the centre of the village, a small triangular green with a sycamore at its centre give Burton Bradstock a focal point of the traditional kind. Around the tree is a battered circular seat whose iron strips must have supported many thousands of Burton bottoms since it was erected. An inscription tells us it was presented to the parish by Mrs Gillett in 1902 "as a memorial to Queen Victoria and in commemoration of the coronation of King Edward VII".

ABOVE: BURTON BRADSTOCK

The churchyard at Burton Bradstock. Nine hundred years ago the village was called Bridetun – the farm on the River Bride. The stream rises at Little Bredy and flows through much of south-west Dorset to reach the sea at Burton Freshwater, the western end of the Chesil Beach. The later addition of "Bradstock" comes from the Wiltshire abbey of Bradenstoke, which owned the manor from the 13th century.

OPPOSITE: THORNCOMBE

From the top of Fore Street, the road slopes sharply away to give Thorncombe a main street which must be the steepest in Dorset. The village is built on a hillside and its tumbling streams and clusters of cottages are more reminiscent of Devon than Dorset. Thorncombe is close to the border with Devon (and Somerset) and was part of it until a boundary change in 1842. In the 18th century Thorncombe produced two famous sons. Samuel and Alexander Hood both became Admirals and peers of the realm — Viscounts Hood and Bridport. They were also friends of Nelson, who described Samuel as the best officer in England.

ABOVE: THORNCOMBE

At the corner of Fore Street and Chard Street is a public water tap, provided in 1902 and happily still in working order. "This supply of drinking water for the people of Thorncombe was planned by William Herbert Evans of Forde Abbey in whose memory it is laid on," says the inscription. Legend tells us it was at Thorncombe 850 years ago that Alice, Viscountess of Devon, came face to face with a party of monks trudging sadly through the village with their cross. They told her they had left Waverley Abbey in Surrey nine years earlier to colonise a new abbey in Devon. But recently their benefactor had died and they faced starvation unless they could get back to Waverley. As it happened, Alice was none other than the sister and heiress of the monks' benefactor and she offered them Thorncombe Manor to stay in and land on which to build an abbey. The manor house has long since disappeared but Forde Abbey survives two miles away as one of the finest and oldest buildings in Dorset.

ABOVE: **THORNCOMBE**

A terrace of stone cottages in High Street, Thorncombe.

ABOVE: BETTISCOMBE

Bettiscombe squats unobtrusively on the northern side of the lush green Marshwood Vale in West Dorset, a modest little community comprising church, manor house, farm and a handful of cottages. The church, St Stephen's, is built in chert and was rebuilt (with original Norman tower and windows) in 1862 to the plans of John Hicks, the Dorchester architect to whom the 16-year-old Thomas Hardy was apprenticed six years earlier. The brick-built manor house dates from about 1694.

ABOVE: NETHERBURY

St Mary's Church stands high on a hillside overlooking the rooftops of Netherbury village below. It was restored in the 19th century but is mostly medieval with a high tower and a Purbeck marble font used in christenings for upwards of 800 years. The pulpit is almost four centuries old and unusually fine with Corinthian columns and carvings in abundance.

Above: **NETHERBURY**

The churchyard at Netherbury. Inside the church, the monuments include the battered alabaster figure of a 15th century knight in armour and brasses to members of the seafaring Hood family, cousins of the Admirals Hood of Thorncombe. The Netherbury branch included another Samuel – Admiral Sir Samuel Hood, who served under Nelson at Santa Cruz, the Nile and Rochefort; another Alexander, who sailed with Captain Cook and died in battle in 1798; and their brother Arthur, yet another naval man, who drowned in the West Indies in 1775.

Opposite: **NETHERBURY**

Netherbury is an unusually hilly village, or "uplandish", as John Leland described it centuries ago. It is also a large village and boasted a population of 2,000 when Queen Victoria came to the throne. Many earned a wage from flax growing, formerly a major branch of agriculture in this valley, which supplied the rope industry at Bridport. Most of the houses here are of the distinctive yellow stone provided by local quarries.

ABOVE: **BROADWINDSOR**

A plaque on the wall of King Charles Cottage at Broadwindsor tells us that "King Charles II slept here" on the night of September 23-24, 1651. In fact, he probably slept very little, as he was being pursued by Parliamentary troops who arrived at the Castle Inn half-an-hour after he did, unaware that their quarry was in the same building. The king escaped largely as a result of a woman, attached to a large band of Parliamentarian camp followers, who happened to give birth that very night. The original Castle Inn was burnt down in 1856.

Above: BROADWINDSOR

Broadwindsor from the churchyard. The village has a small square featuring pub, Post Office, telephone box, some appealing stone cottages and, close by, a large church. This has Norman origins and a 15th century tower but underwent major restoration in 1868. The pulpit is 16th century and was preached from in the 17th by the Royalist author and poet Thomas Fuller, who wrote *The History of the Holy Warre* and *The Worthies of England*. He was rector from 1634 to 1650, when he was replaced by a local Puritan, John Pinney. The living returned to Fuller in 1660 but he admired the interloper and graciously allowed Pinney's eloquent sermons to continue.

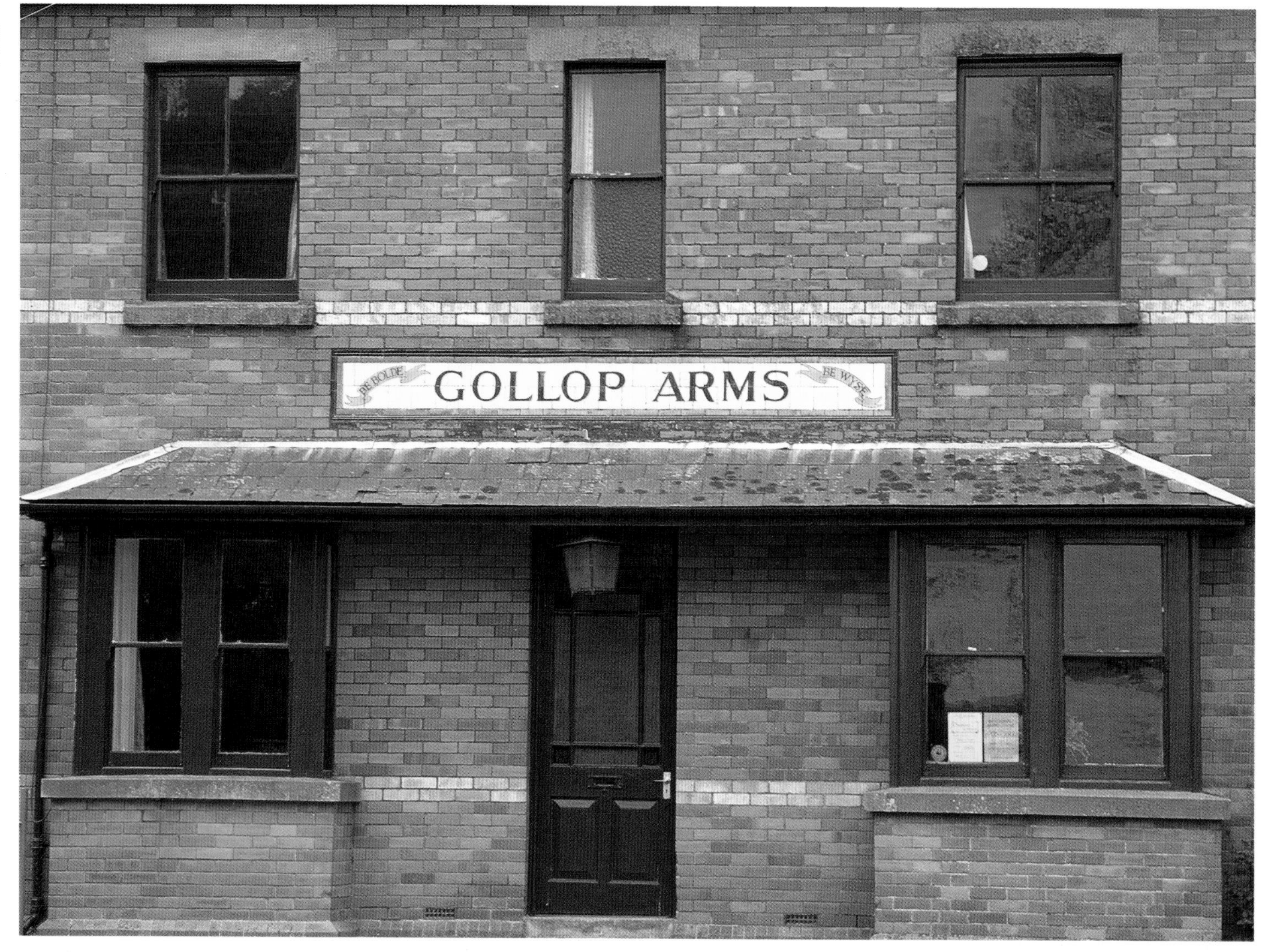

ABOVE: SOUTH BOWOOD

An imposing but perhaps slightly incongruous building in the green depths of rural West Dorset is the Gollop Arms at South Bowood near Stoke Abbott. It stands beside the Broadwindsor to Bridport road, its dark red brick walls and slate tiled roof contrasting starkly with the yellow stone which is the usual building material around here. It was built in 1921 to replace another pub which had burnt down. The pub closed about 1980, since when the building has been a private house. But its pub name remains, set in tiles above the door, and owners Bob and Vee Driscoll are still occasionally asked about opening time!

ABOVE: STOKE ABBOTT

Peeping out from behind a farmyard is the tower of St Mary's Church, Stoke Abbott, built in Norman times and remodelled and probably lengthened in the 13th century. Many of its early English windows have survived and, despite restoration of the nave in 1878, it remains, as Sir Frederick Treves wrote in 1906, "a graceful type of the simple village church of long ago".

ABOVE: STOKE ABBOTT

Stoke Abbott has a rich variety of cottages ranging from 17th century to Victorian and "all very rural and unassuming", as Jo Draper puts it. Many have thatched roofs with walls of light yellow stone. The approach to St Mary's Church passes this house, which bears the dates 1751 and 1762 but looks decidedly older, not least because of its mullioned windows. One who passed this way often in the 18th century was the poet William Crowe, who was rector here from 1782-87. He is best remembered for his poem on nearby Lewesdon Hill, one of the highest hills in Dorset at 894 feet. The verse was admired by two better known poets, Wordsworth and Coleridge, who also knew the area well.

OPPOSITE: NORTH POORTON

Like many communities in West Dorset, North and South Poorton are small, rural and remote. They consist of a handful of thatched cottages with stone walls and thatched roofs. North Poorton also has a church, dedicated to St Mary Magdalene and completely rebuilt by John Hicks in 1861-2. He included stone from the original church in the lower parts of the walls. This 'redevelopment' angered Monica Hutchings when she came here in the 1960s. "Upon going into these little Dorset churches and realising what the Victorians have irrevocably destroyed for us I have realised the full enormity of their crimes," she wrote. "In their haste to bring things up to date — their date — they threw out the old and replaced it with hygienic, durable furnishings."

ABOVE: POWERSTOCK

Powerstock's roots are lost in the mists of history, as are the origins of its name, more correctly spelt Poorstock, as in neighbouring North and South Poorton. William the Conqueror's Domesday Book took this one step further with a Norman translation (Povrestoch) in 1086. The village sits amid knolls and dells, surrounded by prehistoric places like Eggardon hillfort and historic ones like the site of King Athelstan's palace, now a simple green mound called the Castle.

OPPOSITE: POWERSTOCK

Overlooking the lesser knolls of Powerstock from its own higher one is St Mary's Church, possessing the most elaborately decorated Norman chancel arch in Dorset. There is also a fine 15th century door, flanked by two figures, one crowned and bearded with a book in one hand and a staff in the other, the second a young woman, also crowned, with a small child at her side and a loaf of bread in each hand. The figures are thought to represent King Wenceslas and St Elizabeth, Princess of Hungary.

ABOVE: WYNFORD EAGLE

The only eagle here is a stone one perched on the roof of the Manor House, rebuilt in 1830. The village takes the second part of its name from the family of Gilbert del Egle, its Norman owners, who came from Laigle in France. The modest church of St Lawrence, rebuilt in 1840 "in rather mean manner", as Jo Draper puts it, stands alone.

ABOVE: WYNFORD EAGLE

From 1551 Wynford Eagle was home to the Sydenham family, who produced one famous son and one infamous. The former was Thomas, a great 17th century physician, described by Sir Frederick Treves as "the father of British medicine — he threw aside the jargon and ridiculous traditions with which medicine was then hampered, and applied to the study of it sound common sense,". The infamous son was William, the last male of the line, who tried to solve his financial problems by offering his ancestral estate in a lottery. The result was fixed, of course; except that the pre-arranged 'winner', who had agreed to give up her prize for a reward, reneged on the deal while Sydenham refused to give up the manor and ended his days in Dorchester Jail.

ABOVE: LITTLE BREDY

One of the prettiest villages in Dorset is Little Bredy, nestling unobtrusively at the head of the Bride Valley. The River Bride itself rises from the chalk in the landscaped grounds of Bridehead, the manor house rebuilt in the 1830s, to flow at a suitably leisurely pace through the village.

ABOVE: LITTLE BREDY

Little Bredy was extensively remodelled and landscaped in the 1830s and '40s and St Michael's Church (background of picture) and most of the thatched stone cottages date from this period. Even the village hall (foreground) is disguised as a cottage, though it was originally a school. These buildings are a little way down the slope. At the bottom the cottages stand at respectful distances from each other and the Bride's clear waters trickle noisily under a small stone bridge. Beyond this, the terrain slopes steeply upwards once again and the cottages abruptly give way to rich green woodland.

RIGHT: LITTLE BREDY

Little Bredy is described by Newman and Pevsner as "a delightful essay in picturesque estate housing, owing much to Nash's Blaise Hamlet, but more complex and diffuse". It is built partly on a hillside and motorists are discouraged from taking their vehicles beyond the octagonal shelter which marks the descent into the most picturesque parts of the village.

ABOVE: **ASKERSWELL**

Askerswell was called Oscherwille in the Domesday Book of 1086, Oskereswell in a document dated 1201 and Askereswell in 1208. "Spring or stream belonging to a man called Osgar" is A. D. Mills' interpretation. Osgar's stream today wends its way through a village of farm buildings, stone cottages, modern bungalows and narrow lanes, all set in a valley a short distance from the Bridport-Dorchester road. Askerswell is an ancient village, boasting an Iron Age farmstead and a church, St Michael's, of medieval origin but rebuilt in 1858.

ABOVE: ABBOTSBURY

Abbotsbury is a picture-postcard village with an abundance of thatched yellow-stone cottages and an abnormal range of attractions which have made it one of the most visited places in Dorset. The most famous of these is the swannery, founded by monks at least 600 years ago (and probably longer) to provide a regular source of food. The monastery itself is almost 1,000 years old, pre-dating the Norman conquest by 20 or 30 years. It was founded by a Viking couple called Orc and Tola. Orc was steward to both King Canute and Edward the Confessor.

ABOVE: ABBOTSBURY

Apart from St Catherine's Chapel and the remains of a couple of gateways, the old Tithe Barn (pictured) is the only survivor of the original abbey buildings. It was built about 1400 and is one of the largest barns in England, measuring 272 feet from end to end, though only half remains intact and is now in use as a country museum. Abbotsbury's other attractions include an Iron Age fort called Abbotsbury Castle, twenty sheltered acres of sub-tropical gardens and, high on a hill, 14th century St Catherine's Chapel, where spinsters once went to pray for a husband. The abbey church has long since disappeared but the parish church of St Nicholas is of interest, not least because of the holes in and around the pulpit, made by musket fire during a six-hour battle between Royalists and attacking Parliamentarians in 1644.

ABOVE: PORTESHAM

Portesham – often spelt Portisham – is known as the village where Nelson's Hardy spent his boyhood before going to sea at the age of 12. It sits in a hollow in the downs, described by Treves in 1906 as a "somewhat dull settlement, although cheered by a clear and rapid rivulet which chatters down the street". The same stream runs beneath the cottage in the picture. Thomas Masterman Hardy was born three or four miles away at Kingston Russell but moved to Portesham as a nine-year-old and always referrred to it affectionately as "Possum". He became Nelson's flag-captain and his name was the last word that the dying Admiral spoke: "God bless you, Hardy." A mile from Portesham, on Hardy's land at Blackdown, is the famous 80-foot Hardy Monument erected in his memory on a hill 700 feet above sea level.

ABOVE: FRAMPTON

Frampton means literally a farm or estate on the River Frome. It is an extremely old village and the remains of both ancient British and Roman settlements have been found here. The Frome runs through a well-wooded park which has outlived its manor house, built in 1704 and demolished in 1935. The village is curiously imbalanced with cottages on one side of the road, park on the other. Some blame this on the demolition work of a Victorian squire keen to extend his park, others on a plumber who started a fire which destroyed 43 cottages in 1796.

OPPOSITE: MAIDEN NEWTON

Few spots in Dorset provide a more charming vignette than the Old Mill at Maiden Newton, now restored as a picturesque private house spanning the Frome. The main building has three main storeys plus attic and both it and the adjoining outbuilding retain overhanging "lucoms" – extended dormers with trapdoors designed to put the sack hoist beyond the wall of the building and to protect it from the elements. The village centre is marked by the stump of a 15th century cross which once featured fine carvings. Most of the structure was removed when the village found itself on a main coaching route in the 18th century.

ABOVE: SYDLING ST NICHOLAS

Sydling St Nicholas's position on a road to nowhere has helped it maintain a reputation as one of the loveliest villages in Dorset. Even the hideous confluence of telegraph wires seen here detracts only slightly from the general beauty of the place. It is surrounded by hills from which flows the Sydling Water, dividing into three streams as it passes through the village, as a result of which many cottages are reached by little bridges. Some cottages are built of brick and flint, others of stone and flint, others of cob, and many are thatched.

ABOVE: SYDLING ST NICHOLAS

Longfellow's poem *The Village Blacksmith* could have been written for Sydling St Nicholas, for the place possesses just such a "spreading chestnut tree" as the one under which the poet's smithy stood. It was planted as recently as 1911, however, 29 years after Longfellow's death, and still thrives beside a crossroads at the southern end of the village. The battered remains of an old stone cross survive a few yards from the tree. This was a popular meeting place in the past and the site of St Nicholas's Fair, held each year on December 6.

ABOVE: NETHER CERNE

Nether Cerne's church, manor house and cottages stand in a close-knit group on the bank of the Cerne, presenting a placid picture of rural togetherness. At one time the disused Church of All Saints was neglected and overgrown but the care and attention of the Redundant Churches Fund has now enabled it to grow old gracefully. "It is a picturesque building of the 13th century, in a charming pastoral setting," says their gazetteer. It is built of flint and stone and was refashioned in the 15th century. Nether Cerne House dates from the 17th and 18th.

ABOVE: UPCERNE MANOR

"The River haveing left Wolton immediatelie crosseth another Brooke, that cometh down by Upcearne, where Sir Robert Meller, nowe Lorde of it, hath built a House." The house was Upcerne Manor and the reference to it was made by Thomas Gerard, the father of Dorset topography, in about 1623, when the gabled house was a new addition to the central Dorset landscape. Today it is an old timer, much altered in the 19th and 20th centuries but still an architectural gem with its mullioned windows and tiny church adjacent. Its ingredients include stone fragments probably gathered from the ruins of Cerne Abbey.

ABOVE: UPCERNE

Upcerne sits in a bowl in the chalk downlands, "smiling to itself like a child in hiding, delighted that the highroad passes so near yet misses it", as Arthur Mee put it in 1939. He added that "the great world passes it by", as indeed it still does to a very great extent.

OPPOSITE: UPCERNE

Upcerne's rural beatuy is accentuated by the contrast between the richly-wooded parkland of its immediate environs and the relatively bare hillsides which surround it. On one hill is the Cross and Hand, an oval stone pillar, three-and-a-half feet high and thought to be a boundary marker from Roman or Saxon times, though opinions on its purpose vary.

ABOVE: CERNE ABBAS

Cerne Abbas was a small town until the 19th century, when depopulation and the decline of local industries reduced it to its present village status. It remains blessed with an ample share of historical assets, however, including scattered remnants of the Abbey buildings and farm, a fine 15th century church, street frontages covering 500 years of architectural tastes and styles and the mysterious hillside giant whose great chalk frame is probably older than anything in the village below. The Abbey was founded 80 years before the arrival of William the Conqueror and spawned the market town which flourished until 150 years ago.

ABOVE: CERNE ABBAS

A curtain of Virginia creeper makes a magnificent autumnal display on the gabled wall of the Royal Oak in Long Street, Cerne Abbas. The listed building dates from the 1540s and features some excellent stonework looted from the abandoned abbey following the dissolution of the monasteries. The inn sign depicts Charles II's escape from capture by hiding in a hollow oak in 1651, the event which gave this and many other pubs their name. Inside, the free house has other virtues, including axed and moulded beams in the central section of the bar.

ABOVE: MINTERNE MAGNA

St Andrew's Church is 17th century with a tower built in 1800. It stands beside the main road through the village, so close that the tower is almost on the highway. Nearby is Minterne House, the Edwardian manor house built in 1904-6 for the 10th Lord Digby and designed by Leonard Stokes. It was the architect's only commission of this kind and he produced what Newman and Pevsner consider to be "a beautifully sophisticated design, executed throughout in Ham Hill ashlar". Minterne Magna is surrounded on all sides by rolling hills, among them High Stoy, which rises to 860 feet to provide fine views across North Dorset, Wiltshire and Somerset. The village pump (right) is a reminder of the days when villagers drew their water from the well below, now filled in. George King, retired carpenter on Lord Digby's estate, remembers helping to make the wooden casing as an apprentice in 1930. "We used oak from a mill which was pulled down at Minterne Parva," he said. "It replaced an earlier pump and we were very proud of it. But it has never been used as a pump in my time."

PREVIOUS PAGE: HILLFIELD

The parish church of St Nicholas, Hillfield, is one of the smallest in England. Its situation is rather isolated, some distance from the nearest houses and the famous Hillfield Friary, founded after World War I to house and train men in need of help. The church's origins are medieval but it underwent a major restoration in 1848 after falling into disrepair. Inside, features include carved bench ends of uncertain date, many featuring Biblical scenes.

ABOVE: BATCOMBE

Batcombe, like Hillfield, occupies the middle ground between the clay lowlands of North Dorset and the chalk uplands which run in a broad diagonal swathe across the centre of the county. It perches on the very slopes of Batcombe Hill, where the chalk begins. St Mary's Church, built of flint and rubble, is closest of all to the bare green hillside and before the turn of the century was missing one of the four pinnacles from its tower. Legend blames the loss on Conjuror Minterne, a 17th century squire noted for his dealings with the devil. It's said a horse's trailing hoof removed the pinnacle as the mounted Minterne leapt from the crest of the hill intending to clear the church at the bottom.

ABOVE: RAMPISHAM

Edwardian writer Sir Frederick Treves described Rampisham as one of the most beautiful villages in Dorset, "a place of old thatched cottages, with a tiny, creeper-clad inn of great antiquity". Little has changed. It still stands beside a stream in a wooded valley with its thatched Post Office and store (pictured), its church, Jacobean manor house and unusually-named pub, the Tiger's Head. In the churchyard is the hefty stump of a 15th century preaching cross with worn but elaborately-carved figures depicting the stoning of Stephen and other scenes. A Roman tesselated pavement was discovered at Rampisham in 1799, sadly a century or two too soon, for it attracted more thoughtless treasure seekers than kid-gloved excavators and was quickly destroyed. Rampisham is pronounced "Ransom" and a story is told of an outing by the church choir to sing in another village. On arrival they heard the resident choir in full voice, singing "The year of jubilee has come, Return ye ransomed sinners home." Mistaking "ransomed sinners" for "Rampisham singers", the offended choristers turned on their heels and headed for home without a note passing their lips.

ABOVE: EVERSHOT

Evershot is the second highest village in Dorset, perching in a hollow in the hills some 650 feet above sea level. Here Dorset's second river — and the biggest that can claim to belong exclusively to the county — begins its 35-mile journey to the sea. It rises as St John's spring to become the gently-flowing Frome, meandering towards Maiden Newton and Dorchester, then on to Wool and Wareham where it enters Poole Harbour.

OPPOSITE: EVERSHOT

Evershot is the Evershead of Thomas Hardy's Wessex novels and it was here that Tess of the d'Urbervilles had breakfast "at a cottage by the church". The building in question is the thatched stone cottage on the church's western side (see picture). Other Hardy works refer to the Sow-and-Acorn, which survives today as the Acorn Inn. Evershot remains a fairly big village and boasts a remarkable range of architecture in its street scene, including 17th and 18th century cottages and some Victorian imitations. More imitation can be found in St Osmund's Church but the tower and north arcade are genuine 15th century.

Above: MELBURY OSMOND

Legend tells us that the ill-fated Duke of Monmouth took refuge in a cottage at Melbury Osmond after his defeat at Sedgemoor by the forces of his uncle, James II. Thomas Hardy borrowed the tale for his short story *The Duke's Reappearance*, rechristening the village King's Hintock in this and other works, including *The Woodlanders*. Hardy himself had a personal link with Melbury Osmond for his parents were married here in 1839.

Opposite: MELBURY OSMOND

Treves described Melbury Osmond as "the most charming village in these western backwoods". Ninety years later it remains unspoilt and picturesque with a pretty watersplash and a fine collection of thatched stone cottages. St Osmond's Church has medieval origins but was completely rebuilt in 1745 after falling into a "ruinous" condition. Its past clergy include the Rev John Biddell, who after his death in 1732 was described as "a person of such universal goodness that 'tis difficult to single out any virtue in which he was more particularly eminent". No less saintly was parishioner Mary Ainslie (died 1757), whose husband of 21 years "never saw her once ruffled with anger or heard her utter a peevish word".

ABOVE: WEST HILL, NEAR SHERBORNE

Attractive West Hill Cottage is a 19th century toll-house two miles south-east of Sherborne, where the roads to Blandford and Dorchester divide. It is referred to as Sherton Turnpike in Hardy's *Far From the Madding Crowd*. It is here that the pursuing Oak and Coggan catch up with Bathsheba's pony and trap, which they believe has been stolen by gipsies. In fact the driver turns out to be Bathsheba herself on a clandestine journey to Bath.

ABOVE: RYME INTRINSICA

Ryme Intrinsica has the prettiest place-name in Dorset, though the village itself is not quite as pretty as it sounds nor the explanation as poetic. Ryme comes from the Old English rima, meaning a "rim, edge or border" and probably refers to its situation near the county boundary with Somerset or on the slope of a ridge. Intrinsica means "lying within the bounds", distinguishing this "home" part of the manor of Ryme from the outer part, Ryme Extrinsica, at Long Bredy. The village has some pleasing stone cottages and a church dating from the 13th century. It is one of only two in England dedicated to St Hypolite (died AD 236), a Roman jailor converted to Christianity by one of his charges, St Lawrence.

RIGHT: OBORNE

Oborne was called Womburnan in 975, Wocburne in 1086 and Woburn in 1212 before becoming Oburne in a document of 1479. The name comes from the Old English "woh" and "burna" meaning a place "at the crooked or winding stream". The stream in question is the River Yeo. Oborne's present church was built in 1862 but the chancel of an earlier building survives in the care of the Redundant Churches Fund, who describe it as one of the last pre-Reformation churches built. Buried here in 1778 was Robert Goadby, publisher of the *Sherborne Mercury*, ancestor of the *Western Gazette*.

ABOVE: TRENT

Trent's most famous visitor was King Charles II, who hid here for three weeks after defeat at Worcester in 1651. To avert suspicion he disguised himself as a servant and attended a service in St Andrew's Church. Trent is a village without a recognisable centre but with an impressive number of old stone buildings from the 15th, 16th and 17th centuries. The jewels in the crown are the church and adjoining Chantry (pictured), the latter probably built as a priest's house in about 1500. The church is one of the few in Dorset with a spire projecting from its slender early 14th century tower.

OPPOSITE: SANDFORD ORCAS

A gem among Dorset manor houses is Sandford Orcas Manor, built in the reign of Henry VIII and little changed in 450 years. "A complete, small manor house, a fine piece of architecture in itself, and very little altered," say Newman and Pevsner. It is built of Ham Hill stone with features that include four-centred arches for both carriages and pedestrians. It also enjoys continuity of ownership (the Medlycotts have been there for 250 years) and a reputation for hauntings unrivalled in Dorset. The house stands next to the medieval church of St Nicholas.

ABOVE: STOURTON CAUNDLE

Stourton Caundle is one of several "Caundle" villages in North Dorset's Blackmore Vale but how they came by the name is uncertain. There is no mystery about the prefix "Stourton", however — this was the name of the family that held the manor from the 15th century. Before their time the village was called Caundle Haddon after an earlier lord of the manor. Stourton Caundle has some fine stone buildings, a 13th century church and the nave of a chapel which is all that survives of the Stourton family's fortified manor.

ABOVE: KING'S STAG

King's Stag gives us the legend of Henry III and a white hart that he met while hunting. The creature's beauty so impressed him that he spared it and ordered others to do likewise. But the forest bailiff fell foul of the warning, killing the hart on the bridge over the River Lydden, for which he was severely punished. King's Stag is said to derive its name from the incident but place-name experts offer something less romantic. Mills says the boundaries of three parishes meet on the bridge and that King's Stag really means "king's stake or boundary post". The miniature black and white church (pictured) was built in 1914 by a Bishop of Worcester in memory of his wife Lady Barbara Yeatman-Biggs.

ABOVE: OKEFORD FITZPAINE

Okeford Fitzpaine is called Oakford-Fitzpiers in Hardy's *The Woodlanders* but it is known colloquially as Fippenny Ockford. An ancient legend tells of a tragic fire in a neighbouring village and a collection to help an orphaned child. Fippenny Ockford gave five pence, Sixpenny Handley sixpence and Shilling Okeford (Shillingstone) a shilling. This, the story tells us, is how the villages came by their names while the child's own parish became Child Okeford. Inevitably the truth is less romantic. Okeford Fitzpaine takes its name from the Fitzpaine family, Shillingstone from the Schelins and Child Okeford from the Old English "cild" meaning "son of a royal or noble family".

OPPOSITE: OKEFORD FITZPAINE

In the 18th and early 19th centuries Okeford was a great smuggling centre, home of the notorious Roger Ridout, a maternal ancestor of the author. Ridout was the village miller but he also led a smuggling gang which brought wagonloads of contraband from the coast to nearby Fiddleford Mill, where it was stored in outhouses. Ridout was tried for murder (and acquitted) and jailed for smuggling but he lived to be 75 and is buried in St Andrew's churchyard.

ABOVE: OKEFORD FITZPAINE

Okeford Fitzpaine is quite a large village and a very pretty one with a fine crop of 18th century cottages, many in local red brick, some with timber framing. Newman and Pevsner describe it as "unusually coherent, with almost nothing out of scale or in other ways striking a false note". The 15th century church tower is regarded as an oddity as it includes the window and arch of its 14th century predecessor which would normally have been demolished.

ABOVE: CHILD OKEFORD

Child Okeford is another large village, with a mix of modern and older buildings grouped around the church and war memorial. It sits under Hambledon Hill, an Iron Age hillfort and the site of a famous incident during the English Civil War. This was the last stand of the Clubmen, an army of country people sick of seeing their crops trampled and livestock plundered by the soldiers of Parliament and the King. They banded together in their thousands and, armed with clubs and pitchforks, resolved to take on both sides. They were soundly defeated by Cromwell's army in August 1645. "We have taken about 300, many of which are poor silly creatures," he wrote of his latest prisoners-of-war.

ABOVE: HAMMOON

The 13th century St Paul's Church, Hammoon, and, in the background, the manor house which Treves described as "the most picturesque of its kind". Most of the house is 17th century but it has a fine porch and two-storey bay window of the late 16th. Hammoon means "enclosure or river meadow of the Moyon family". They came from Normandy and held the manor soon after the conquest. It is a small village grouped neatly around a crossroads on the west bank of the Stour. It is also very quiet with little through traffic and a railway line that closed 30 years ago.

OPPOSITE: HINTON ST MARY

Hinton St Mary is another village on the River Stour and had its own flour mill well into the present century. As Jo Draper observes, visitors should leave the main road to see the best of the village, including St Peter's Church with its 15th century tower, the manor house with its 17th century facade, a tithe barn built about 1500 but altered in the 1930s and many attractive stone cottages, some still thatched. In 1963 an exceptionally fine Roman mosaic pavement featuring the head of Christ was found at Hinton. It is now in the British Museum.

ABOVE: **MARNHULL**

On the west side of Marnhull church is Senior's Farm, the oldest house in the village, probably built about 1500 as a grange of Glastonbury Abbey. The beams in the house and barn contain oak nails up to one foot long. A painting on a wooden screen is said to be a portrait of Edward VI. A stone's throw from here is another historic building, the Crown Inn, used by Thomas Hardy as the model for the Pure Drop in *Tess of the Durbervilles*. Tess herself was born in the village, which Hardy called Marlott.

OPPOSITE: **MARNHULL**

The church of St Gregory at Marnhull contains elements from the 14th century, but much of it dates only from Victorian times, when it was substantially rebuilt and extended. According to Hutchins, the 15th century tower "fell down about 1718 during divine service"; but this is an exaggeration, for the collapse involved only the top section of the south face. A former parish clerk here was John Warren (died in 1752, aged 94) who, according to his memorial, "smoked all his life/And so did his wife/But now there's no doubt/But their pipes are both out"!

Above: IWERNE MINSTER

Red-brick half-timbered houses are a speciality of Iwerne Minster. Most date from the late-Victorian period, when a local squire, the 2nd Lord Wolverton, initiated a spate of building in this style. The transformation was still going on when Treves was writing his *Highways and Byways* book in the early 1900s. "The low thatched cottages are gradually vanishing, to be replaced by bold houses of gaudy brick and tiles," he wrote. Dating from the same era is Clayesmore School, designed for Lord Wolverton by Alfred Waterhouse in 1878 and decribed by Newman and Pevsner as "the most ambitious high Victorian mansion" in Dorset.

Right: IWERNE MINSTER

Unlike most villages, Iwerne Minster has managed to preserve its village pump since Victorian times. It carries the date 1880 and occupies a little shelter built later by another village squire, James Ismay, as a place where people could gather to read the latest news of the First World War. Ismay bought the Iwerne estate in 1908 and created a "model village" atmosphere, with hand-painted shop signs, various agricultural experiments and specially-designed clothes for the children.

ABOVE: FARNHAM

White-painted thatched cottages built — unusually — with their gable ends to the highway contribute to the aesthetic attractions of Farnham, a village of Cranborne Chase and the Dorset-Wiltshire border country. At the turn of the century Farnham was world famous, attracting up to 40,000 visitors a year to its Larmer Tree grounds and the museum founded by the father of archaeology, General Pitt-Rivers. The museum has long since closed but the inn which accommodated many of the visitors survives as the Museum Hotel. Two hundred years ago this was also smuggling country and the scene of a famous battle between smugglers and soldiers.

ABOVE: **FONTMELL MAGNA**

While Iwerne Minster specialises in brick and timber houses, typical materials of its neighbour Fontmell Magna are brick and flint, with thatched roofs in some cases. St Andrew's Church – described as "large and lavish" by Newman and Pevsner – dates mostly from 1862 but part of the tower is medieval. In the churchyard is a memorial to Philip Salkeld, a rector's son posthumously awarded the VC for his heroism during the Indian Mutiny in 1857. Nearby is the Fontmell Brook, which heads west from here to join the River Stour near Hammoon.

ABOVE: ASHMORE

Ashmore is a delightful village and, at 700 feet above sea level, the highest one in Dorset. It sits high in the green and wooded hills of Cranborne Chase, clustered around a pond which was its lifeblood for centuries and now combines with some fine stone and thatched buildings to present a picture postcard image. A tradition here is the Filly Loo, a ceremony of midsummer merrymaking led by a band playing from a wagon pushed out into the pond. Roland Gant suggests it has something to do with magic and water (l'eau).

ABOVE: ASHMORE

Ashmore takes its name from the Old English words "aesc" and "mere", meaning "Pool where ash trees grow". The pond is 75 yards in diameter and probably the oldest feature of the village as well as the best-known. It certainly pre-dates the Domesday Book of 1086 (which calls the village Aisemare) and may date back to Roman times or earlier. It rarely dries up and remains Ashmore's greatest asset, supporting a thriving duck population and attracting a constant trickle of visitors who sense something of old England in this peaceful setting.

OPPOSITE: STOURPAINE

Only the River Stour and the disused Somerset and Dorset railway line stand between Stourpaine and Durweston, which gaze fondly at each other across the green valley like mutual admirers who are destined never to meet. Stourpaine is bisected by the main Blandford to Shaftesbury road and saves its best for those who bother to wander a few yards off the beaten track. To the west side they will find a selection of Victorian buildings and older thatched cottages grouped around Holy Trinity Church, largely rebuilt in 1858 but with a fine 15th century greensand tower.

Above: DURWESTON

Durweston occupies the middle ground between gently-sloping hills and the water meadows of the Stour valley. It was called Derwinestone in the Domesday Book, which according to Mills means a "farm belonging to Deorwine", an Old English personal name. The village had three vineyards in those days. The church of St Nicholas has a 15th century tower but the rest was rebuilt in 1846. Many of the houses were built as estate cottages by the Portman family of Bryanston. They also built the solid stone bridge over the Stour, dated 1795 and much mauled by traffic in recent decades.

Opposite: WINTERBORNE STICKLAND

In the distant past Dorset had at least 20 Winterbourne villages, of which about 14 survive as recognisable communities today. Each takes the first part of its name from a stream which runs only (or most strongly) in winter, in this case the River Winterborne or North Winterborne. Dorset also has a South Winterborne, which gives its name to several villages near Dorchester. Winterborne Stickland has a mix of modern houses, Victorian villas and thatched cottages. The centre is picturesque, with a landscaped green divided by the stream, two prominent lime trees (one by the green, the other near the church), the stump of a stone cross and an elaborately carved wooden cross dated 1988.

OPPOSITE: WINTERBORNE WHITECHURCH

Winterborne Whitechurch has some famous connections, most notably with the founder of Methodism, John Wesley, whose father Samuel was born here and whose grandfather was rector in the mid-17th century. It was also the birthplace of the Elizabethan poet George Turberville, who went to Russia as Ambassador's secretary and described the natives as "a people passing rude, to vices vile inclined"! St Mary's Church includes a 13th century chancel.

OPPOSITE: BINGHAM'S MELCOMBE

St Andrew's Church is 14th century and stands in the grounds of Bingham's Melcombe. Both church and house have long since been deserted by their medieval village and now have only each other for company. In the 18th century the church hosted the marriage of John Hutchins, author of the monumental *History of Dorset*, to Anne Stephens, whose heroism in later life was to save her husband's notes from destruction during the great fire of Wareham. The house dates from 1500 and is a fine example of a small medieval manor house.

Above: MELCOMBE BINGHAM

Melcombe Bingham wins the prize for having the most confusing name in Dorset. It is also known as Melcombe Horsey while Bingham's Melcombe is a manor house a mile from the modern village. In medieval times there were other names including Overmelcombe, Upmelcombe Cearne, Turges Upmelcombe and just plain Melcombe (all for Melcombe Horsey) and Nethermelcombe (for Bingham's Melcombe). The Cearne, Turges and Horsey families all held Higher Melcombe Manor at various times and the Binghams were at Bingham's Melcombe for 600 years. "Melcombe" means "milk valley" from the Old English "meoluc" and "cumb".

Above: MILTON ABBAS

Open green verges and facing rows of white thatched cottages make Milton Abbas one of the most picturesque villages in Dorset — and perhaps in England. Ironically, however, the village owes its picture postcard appearance to the selfish arrogance of an 18th century squire, Lord Milton, later Earl of Dorchester. He was irritated by the proximity of the old town to his own house and, to the digust of his tenants, arranged to have their homes demolished one by one and a new village built on a site which would cause minimal disturbance. The church was built in 1786 and extended 100 years later.

Right: MILTON ABBAS

The central door and arches of the almshouses at Milton Abbas, one of the few buildings to survive the planned demolition of the old town of Middleton in the 1770s and '80s. The almshouses were built in 1674 and originally stood in the old town of Middleton, once a flourishing market community adjoining the medieval abbey. In 1779 they were dismantled stone by stone and re-erected in the new village some distance away.

ABOVE: WINTERBORNE ZELSTON

Winterborne Zelston is the last of the North Winterborne villages and owes the latter part of its name to Henry de Seles, who was here in the 14th century. Before his time it was called Winterborne Maureward after another family. The village is close to the A31 Wimborne to Dorchester road but not close enough to spoil it. Thatched cottages have had a high survival rate among the modern bungalows. There are also double-arched bridges and a duck pond. St Mary's Church is mainly Victorian but has a 15th century tower.

ABOVE: **ALMER**

Almer means "eel pool" in Old English and a pond can still be seen beside the A31 trunk road. So can St Mary's Church with its Norman north aisle and doorway, 14th century tower, and nave and porch rebuilt in the 18th century. Almer also has a small Elizabethan manor house with mullioned windows. Across the main road is the seven-mile brick wall, with its stag and lion gates, which surrounds Charborough Park and a magnificent 17th century mansion. Nearby the historic thatched pub, the World's End, was burnt down in 1991 but has since been rebuilt in a similar style.

ABOVE: SHAPWICK

Dorset writer, the late Monica Hutchings, described Shapwick as a "dead-end village", with roads that go nowhere in particular and no bridge across the River Stour. But it's not an unattractive place and the market cross provides a visible centre to enhance the traditional village atmosphere, despite Newman and Pevsner's comment that it is "nothing but a stump now set upon ironstone steps". There are also some pleasing thatched cottages of brick or cob and a 12th century church, St Bartholomew's, built precariously close to the river and prone to flooding as a result.

RIGHT: SPETISBURY

The view from Crawford Bridge, Spetisbury, of the River Stour as it wends its way steadily south-eastwards. Spetisbury is a linear village, similar in shape to the main road which runs through it and the river beside it. An Iron Age hillfort betrays Spetisbury's prehistoric origins. So do the 80 skeletons found in a defensive ditch at the hillfort when the railway line was cut through here in 1857. They were probably victims of the Roman invasion, as part of a Roman shield was found amongst them.

ABOVE: COWGROVE

One of the oldest houses on the Kingston Lacy Estate, near Wimborne, is the 17th century Court House at Cowgrove. It is one of many historic cottages in the picturesque parish of Pamphill and was recently restored by the National Trust over a five-year period. Its features include an oak framework and wattle and daub walls, comprising clay, earth and dung. The building's original role is uncertain. Historians think it was either the home of a court official or that it replaced a medieval moot as the local courthouse. A roadside duck pond is Cowgrove's most obvious feature but here also are several attractive timber-framed cottages from the 17th and 18th centuries. Most of them now belong to the National Trust, which in 1983 inherited the 16,000-acre Kingston Lacy and Corfe Castle Estates through the will of the Honourable Mr Ralph Bankes. The River Stour also passes through Cowgrove, which lies far enough from main roads and Wimborne to retain its rural character.

ABOVE: **STANBRIDGE**

One of the prettiest cottages in Dorset is Stanbridge Lodge, an ornate thatched dwelling beside the Wimborne to Cranborne road at Stanbridge, or Hinton Parva, as it is also known. Its style is deliberately rustic, with a porch of wood and thatch, leaded windows and six external walls of varying dimensions. It serves as a lodge to nearby Gaunts House. The Royal Commission claims it was built in 1809 and has only an attic room upstairs. But the present tenant, who has lived there since 1940, believes it to date from 1750, adding that it has three first floor bedrooms as well as three rooms downstairs.

ABOVE: WITCHAMPTON

Sir Frederick Treves called Witchampton a "garden hamlet" and one of the most beautiful villages in Dorset. Ninety years later it remains picturesque, with an abundance of thatched and timber-framed cottages. Brick is a popular building material here and the Tudor wing of Abbey House opposite the church is one of the oldest brick buildings in Dorset. The church itself has a 15th century tower. The village is on the west bank of the River Allen, whose clear waters rise from the natural chalk reservoirs a few miles to the north and meet the Stour at Wimborne.

LEFT: GUSSAGE ALL SAINTS

The three Gussage villages are presumed to take their names from the "gushing stream" ("gyssic" in Old English) which rises at Gussage St Andrew and passes through Gussage St Michael and Gussage All Saints before joining the Allen. The last of the trio is also the largest and in Treves' time had "some of the most ancient and primitive thatched cottages" in Dorset. Plenty of these brick and cob dwellings survive, thankfully in a less primitive condition. Newman and Pevsner describe the large church of All Saints as "surprising", as it looks Victorian but is genuinely 14th century.

TOP RIGHT: LONG CRICHEL

The hill referred to in the village name is today called Crichel Down. This piece of chalk downland made headline news in the early 1950s when the Marten family of Crichel House campaigned successfully for the return of land which had been compulsorily taken from them as a Second World War bombing site. The case became a cause célèbre, attracting widespread publicity, questions in the House, the Minister of Agriculture's resignation and a change in the rules on such matters.

RIGHT: LONG CRICHEL

Like much of this chalk down country, the area around Long Crichel has an obvious prehistoric past. Round barrows abound and in 1939 evidence of the extraordinary 4,000-year-old brain operation known as trepanning was discovered. Appropriately, this village and its neighbour More Crichel have two of the oldest place-names in Dorset. The first syllable of "Crichel" comes from the Celtic word "crug", meaning "mound, hill or barrow", to which, says Mills, an explanatory Old English "hill" was added at an early date. The "Long" and "More" prefixes appeared in the 12th or 13th centuries, although the medieval villages were sometimes called Crichel Lucy and Crichel Govis after families who lived there.

ABOVE: LONG CRICHEL

According to Newman and Pevsner, St Mary's Church, Long Crichel, is "a very strange building", and they demand to know who was responsible for it. The tower is 15th century, the rest was built in 1852. That is not unusual but the plan and style were about 12 years behind the times and the handling considerably more so. The nave has no aisles, say the experts, and is really "a Georgian space in Perpendicular form — long, uniform, well-lit — it might be a schoolroom." Records of the late 18th century hint at another side to Long Crichel's history — a side involving the twilight world of smuggling. The trail begins a few miles to the south at Colehill, where a well-known smugglers' route still known as Smugglers Lane leads on through Furzehill and Clap Gate and becomes an unmade track to More and Long Crichel. At Wimborne Minster a memorial to a young man who died in 1798 identifies his father as "Isaac Gulliver of Long Crichel" — unquestionably the great smuggler of that name. And a report from Poole Custom House in 1802 tells us of a luxury schooner owned by a big-time smuggler (almost certainly Gulliver) which was on loan or hired out to Charles Sturt, the owner of Crichel House.

ABOVE: **TARRANT HINTON**

Most people merely glimpse Tarrant Hinton as they flash past on the Blandford to Salisbury road but beyond the busy highway is a pleasant and picturesque village with a number of pretty thatched cottages grouped around a medieval church. The 15th century church tower boasts outrageously large gargoyles and battlements. Inside are even greater treasures, including a wonderful Easter sepulchre, created in the early 16th century and held up as a fine early example of the Italian Renaissance influence, and a contrastingly modern iron and brass lectern presented in 1909.

ABOVE: TARRANT HINTON

Wedgwood Cottage, pictured from Tarrant Hinton churchyard on a frosty morning, has cob and brick walls and an old bread oven which is soon to be restored. In the garden bantam hens roam freely in the traditional manner. The cottage is said to have been owned at one time by the famous Wedgwood pottery family. The deeds have been lost but the story is feasible because the Wedgwoods — including Josiah himself — lived at Eastbury House, Tarrant Gunville, in about 1800. In Gunville church is a memorial to Josiah's son Thomas, a photography pioneer, who died in 1805 aged 34.

ABOVE: TARRANT MONKTON

The Tarrant villages take their names from the Tarrant chalk stream, which rises at Tarrant Gunville and joins the Stour at Tarrant Crawford. The word "Tarrant" is another Celtic river name and an unusual variation of "Trent". It probably meant "trespasser", or "river liable to flooding". Tarrant Monkton is one of eight surviving Tarrant villages but there were originally ten if you include the lost hamlets of Tarrant Antioch (near Tarrant Rawston) and Tarrant Preston, today represented by Preston Farm, south of Tarrant Rushton.

Above: TARRANT MONKTON

Motorists at Tarrant Monkton may cross the River Tarrant by way of a ford or water-splash while pedestrians can use the adjacent packhorse bridge. The bridge – probably 17th century – is precious enough to be a listed structure but the white railings are a modern addition. Originally it had no railings but instead had low parapets in order not to obstruct the hanging packs of the horses as they crossed. The concrete surface in the water-splash is another modern addition. It has pipes under it to carry some of the water, or all of it when the level is low. This arrangement is known to bridge buffs as an "Irish bridge"!

ABOVE: TARRANT MONKTON

Tarrant Monkton has a large proportion of thatched cob-walled cottages, most of which lay along a rectangle of roads bisected by the River Tarrant and its water-meadows. Near the ford and packhorse bridge are All Saints' Church with its 14th century chancel and 15th century tower and the thatched village pub, the Langton Arms, which these days attracts patrons from miles around.

FOLLOWING PAGE: HOLT

Lower Row, in the parish of Holt, where the village pond was restored as a labour of love in the early 1970s by a resident whose cottage overlooked it. An earlier resident was Thomas Frampton, described in a report by the Poole Collector of Customs in 1781 as "a great smuggler". From the same report we learn of Customs officers and soldiers searching cottages and outbuildings in the area. Their only find was a cask of brandy hidden in a haystack at Row and in dislodging it they managed to split it open. The soldiers were later found sitting in a field "much in liquor".

ABOVE: HINTON MARTEL

One of the oddest features of any Dorset village is the large fountain in the centre of Hinton Martel. The present version, starring five strange acquatic creatures and a vast concrete wishing bowl, was unveiled by Dorset's first Miss World, Ann Sidney, in 1965, but an earlier model was here at the time of Sir Frederick Treves' visit in the early 1900s. Never one to dodge an issue, he described it as a "circular basin, in the centre of which is just such a fountain as may be found in a suburban tea-garden or in front of a gaudy Italian villa". His verdict would not be unfair on the current model. In the background is St John's Church, rebuilt in 1870.

ABOVE: WIMBORNE ST GILES

Treves described the almshouses at Wimborne St Giles as "a picture of beautiful and dignified old age" and they have lost none of their dignity in the nine decades since his time. The red-brick range was built in 1624, a gift to the community from village squire Sir Anthony Ashley. It was designed to provide ten one-roomed homes – five on each side of the entrance. The latter is a three-bay stone arcade with an armorial panel above and a wonderful oak door inside.

OPPOSITE: WIMBORNE ST GILES

Few places better encapsulate the essence of old rural England than the picturesque centre of Wimborne St Giles. The church – rebuilt in 1732, remodelled in 1886 and again after a fire in 1908 – adjoins the older almshouses. Opposite is the village green and beyond that the age-old trees which screen from view the ancestral home of the Earls of Shaftesbury and their forbears, lords of the manor for 500 years. Nearby the River Allen's clear waters crash into a shallow millpond behind a fine millhouse built in the 17th century, while across the road the decrepit village stocks remind us of a time when public humiliation was the penalty for petty misdemeanours.

ABOVE: WIMBORNE ST GILES

Tulips make a colourful display in a cottage garden at Wimborne St Giles, a village with its own little niche in the history of English gardening. The same Sir Anthony Ashley who gave the almshouses is credited with introducing the cabbage to England. He would have grown his first specimens in the kitchen garden of St Giles House 400 years ago. He died in 1627 and the grand effigies of himself and his wife in the church have a sphere at their feet which is supposed by some to represent a cabbage!

OPPOSITE: WIMBORNE ST GILES

The father of the English cabbage was also the grandfather of the first Earl of Shaftesbury, Sir Anthony Ashley Cooper. He was born at St Giles in 1621 and served as a Royalist MP for two years before changing sides to become a member of Cromwell's Council of State. Later he opposed Cromwell and after the restoration of the monarchy became Chancellor of the Exchequer and Privy Councillor before falling from favour. Equally famous is the seventh Earl, a champion of the poor and pioneer of social reform in the 19th century. He gave his name to Shaftesbury Avenue in London and his work is commemorated by the statue of Eros.

Above: EDMONDSHAM

The lodge and main entrance gates of Edmondsham House, a fine Elizabethan manor begun a year after the Spanish Armada. As at Wimborne St Giles, brick is the dominant building material at Edmondsham. Most of the houses are on the hill leading out of the village centre towards Verwood. There is also a Victorian pump on the hill with a large wheel to work it and a roof. Further up the hill a one-man pottery marks the revival of what was once an important cottage industry in this area.

ABOVE: HORTON

The folly known as Horton Tower is a well-known landmark but another tower — the one on St Wolfrida's Church (right of picture) — also deserves attention. It has a small spire with work complex enough to prompt speculation that the great architect Sir John Vanbrugh was involved. That is not impossible for it was built in 1722-3, when Vanbrugh was at work on the palatial Eastbury House a few miles away at Tarrant Gunville. Beneath the tower is a memorial to an eccentric village squire, Henry Hastings, who ate oysters twice a day and died aged 99 in 1650. He was a great sportsman whose interest in game was matched only by his weakness for women.

ABOVE: STANPIT

The village of Stanpit – seen here from the Marsh which shares its name – is a nondescript kind of place on the road from Christchurch to Mudeford. A couple of centuries ago a notorious smuggler called John Streeter kept a snuff and tobacco factory here and no doubt processed some of the many cargoes he brought ashore illegally at Mudeford Quay. Stanpit Marsh itself is a saltmarsh which today forms an important nature reserve, popular among migrating birds.

OPPOSITE: MUDEFORD

Lobster pots are always much in evidence on Mudeford Quay, where a traditional fishing village atmosphere co-exists happily with the modern trappings of the tourist trade. Long before the boom in tourism, Mudeford witnessed a boom of a different kind – in smuggling. Contraband carriers came here in vast numbers to collect cargoes from their seafaring accomplices. Three hundred smugglers were involved in one particular landing in 1784. Next day the Royal Navy arrived intent on seizing the smugglers' ships. The result was a three-hour gun battle which left several wounded and a senior naval officer dead.

Above: Wick

Victorian and Edwardian buildings clustered around a triangular green help to give the hamlet of Wick a village atmosphere, despite the proximity of Bournemouth (of which it is part) and, across the water, the busy borough of Christchurch. Unlike Bournemouth, which grew up in the 19th century, Wick is an ancient community, first mentioned in Norman documents 900 years ago. Several 17th and 18th century buildings survive to mingle with the modern bungalows.

Opposite: Wick

Christchurch seen from Wick, a hamlet once described as the last village on the River Stour. Water transport has long been important here and the Wick Ferry has a long history. One ferry service from the Christchurch bank was established in the 19th century by Eli Miller, who charged a halfpenny fare and worked a 17-hour day. Another from Wick was launched by a man called Marshall, who had been forced to give up farmwork after breaking his leg. The holiday trade has helped to keep the ferry service alive to the present day. But the river has also brought its problems — flooding was all too common in the past and so were drownings.

Above: HOLDENHURST

Holdenhurst has been described as "the Mother of Bournemouth", and with some justification, for it existed – and had administrative responsibilities – at least 700 years before Lewis Tregonwell built his celebrated seaside mansion at Bourne. In fact, it existed before William the Conqueror and had a Saxon church, replaced as recently as 1934. In recent decades housing estates and busy roads have encroached to within a stone's throw of Holdenhurst, yet it has retained much of its rural character and still sits proudly and prettily around its village green (right of picture).

ABOVE: THROOP

A mile west of Holdenhurst is the hamlet of Throop, which also dates from Saxon times. It grew up around its watermill which, though no longer functioning, remains a focal point, attracting large numbers of visitors. They flock to enjoy Throop's pleasant rural environment on the outskirts of Bournemouth, whose urban expansion threatens eventually to engulf it. Close to the mill is an old ford called Pigshoot, where Sir Walter Tyrrell is supposed to have crossed the River Stour after allegedly firing the arrow which killed King William Rufus in the New Forest in 1100.

ABOVE: **ST ALBAN'S HEAD**

This windswept headland on the Purbeck coast is more commonly called St Aldhelm's Head and the tiny Norman chapel (right of picture) is dedicated to St Aldhelm, a Saxon bishop of Sherborne, who died in 709. But generations of mariners have called the headland after St Alban, the first British martyr, put to death about 304. It is probably a dispute without end, unlike the less harmless dispute between coastguards and smugglers of 150 years ago. The terrace of white cottages was built for coastguards in 1834 and their presence in coastal areas contributed to the decline of smuggling in the mid-19th century.

OPPOSITE: **WORTH MATRAVERS**

No village says more than Worth Matravers about the historical importance of quarrying in this part of Purbeck. Almost everything here is built of Purbeck stone, not just the cottages and 12th century church but even the duckpond in the village centre, described by Jo Draper as "fearfully neat and tidy"! From the pond can be seen a fine exhibition of strip lynchets carved in the hillsides by medieval farmers. Quarrying is even older, having its origins in the Purbeck marble trade developed first by the Romans and later by the Normans.

ABOVE: CORFE CASTLE

A pair of monolithic Tuscan columns supports an 18th century brick porch at Clealls' Stores in East Street, Corfe Castle. The grocery business has been trading under the same name for at least 130 years. In the Market Square the Greyhound Hotel has a similar porch with three columns and the inscription "IC 1733". A second porch at the Greyhound was bricked in during the 19th century. The Bankes Arms also has a columned porch but dates only from the 1920s, making it a rarity in a place where most buildings are 17th or 18th century.

ABOVE: CORFE CASTLE

Corfe Castle from the A351 road. No place in England has a more natural site for a castle than Corfe, where a steep-sided hillock a few miles inland guards the only cleft in the 12-mile range of Purbeck Hills. There was a fortification of some sort here in Saxon times but the royal castle whose ruins we see today was Norman. The castle was blown apart by order of Parliament in 1646 after a three-year siege during the civil war.

ABOVE: CORFE CASTLE

West Street from a different angle. This was once the main road through Corfe. According to Newman and Pevsner, it "deserves to be explored when one is feeling receptive to every twist and turn, every widening and narrowing, every shift in roof level." The use of Purbeck stone as the almost universal building material is the only concession to uniformity.

OPPOSITE: CORFE CASTLE

A pair of Georgian bow windows at Hatchards' gift shop makes its own contribution to the ancient and varied street scene in West Street, Corfe. Beyond is the 18th century Fox Inn, where the Ancient Order of Purbeck Marblers and Stone Cutters meets each year on Shrove Tuesday to enact its centuries-old traditions. From the Fox, the most recently married stonecutter has to carry a pint of beer to the craftsmen's annual business meeting at the Town Hall. Later a football is kicked to Ower Quay on the shores of Poole Harbour, where a pound of pepper is sprinkled over it. This represents the peppercorn rent which the stoneworkers have paid since 1695 for the right to transport their goods to Ower via Peppercorn Lane.

HATCHARDS
The FOX INN
Garden

ABOVE: KINGSTON

Splashes of Post Office red add colour to the greys and greens of Kingston, near Corfe Castle. The greys are provided by the Purbeck stone. Most of the cottages date from the 19th century, as do both churches, the earlier rebuilt with one or two Norman ingredients in 1833, the later built from scratch in the 1870s more to satisfy the third Lord Eldon's craving for grandeur than the needs of the congregation, who were already adequately catered for.

OPPOSITE: KIMMERIDGE

Kimmeridge sits snugly in a green valley, a mile back from its crumbling cliffs and shaley shore and connected to them by a toll road. The cottages are mostly of limestone and thatch and the modest church, rebuilt around a Norman doorway in 1872, almost masquerades as one of them. In the churchyard a row of gravestones testifies to the hazardous lifestyle of the coastguards posted here in the 19th century in an attempt to stamp out smuggling. Most appear to have died in their mid-20s, either from drowning or through accidents with firearms. All were outlived by the terrace of Coastguard cottages which survives on the clifftop.

ABOVE: STEEPLE

Steeple takes its name from the Old English word "stiepel", meaning "steep place", which presumably refers to the hilly nature of the surrounding terrain. Today's Steeple is tiny, having little besides the basic requirements of church, manor house and farm, but there is evidence of a much larger medieval settlement. St Michael's Church has two unusual assets. In the porch is the carved coat of arms of the local Lawrence family, who were linked by marriage with the ancestors of George Washington and whose stars and stripes are said to have inspired the United States flag. In the vestry is a barrel organ, used to lead the Victorian congregation in their singing and recently restored.

ABOVE: BLACKMANSTON

Blackmanston is merely a farm in the parish of Steeple but it was a village once and there was a Saxon settlement here. The surviving farmhouse also has grander origins, having begun life as an Elizabethan manor house. It nestles unobtrusively in a fertile valley of Kimmeridge clay, sandwiched between two ranges of hills and watered by the humble Corfe River. It is here pictured from the hills above Kimmeridge looking towards the main Purbeck range.

ABOVE: TYNEHAM

The antique telephone box is a star exhibit at Tyneham, where 50 years of military occupation have inadvertently turned an old coastal village into an open air museum. Ironically, the red and white concrete box was considered an eyesore when it appeared in 1928. The engineer who erected it was apparently sworn at by the local rector! By 1943, when Tyneham was taken over by the army, the box was already a rarity. It was restored in the early 1980s.

OPPOSITE: TYNEHAM

The church and school have also been restored and now house permanent exhibitions on the area's archaeology, history, geography, geology and natural history. But the uninhabited ruins of Post Office Row (left) are a sad reminder of the tragedy of Tyneham, a community sacrificed to the national interest. Its people moved out in 1943 believing they would one day return to the homes some families had occupied for generations. "Please treat the church and houses with care," they said in a touching note pinned to the church door. But the villagers were never allowed to return and in their absence Tyneham was reduced to ruin by shellfire and neglect.

ABOVE: **WEST LULWORTH**

Fishing, smuggling and piracy were West Lulworth's primary industries in the past but these days tourism is its lifeblood. Visitors flock here in their thousands, lured by an array of natural and man-made attractions. The star turn is Lulworth Cove, a mile in circumference, created by the erosion of soft sands and clays after the sea carved a gap in the limestone cliffs. The water is said to be the coldest in Dorset due to its depth and the freshwater springs which rise here. In the village itself, the trappings of tourism abound but the road down to the cove has plenty of attractive stone and thatched cottages.

ABOVE: LULWORTH COVE

Lulworth Cove is known as the place where John Keats wrote his last sonnet, and spent his last day in England. He was on his way to Italy in 1820, hoping that the Mediterranean climate might save him from death by consumption. At Lulworth, his ship was becalmed. Keats and his friend went ashore and the scenery so lifted his spirits that on the flyleaf of a volume of Shakespeare he scribbled the last inspired verses he was destined to write. Later he continued to Italy, where he died the following year at the age of 26.

ABOVE: EAST LULWORTH

East Lulworth is three miles from the Cove and a village of two parts. In a fine parkland setting stand two churches and the ruin of Lulworth Castle, built about 1608 and wrecked by fire in 1929. The parish church is St Andrew's, built in the 15th century and rebuilt in 1788 and again in 1864. Nearby is St Mary's, a Roman Catholic chapel built for the Weld family in 1786-7, apparently with George III's express permission. In the village itself, most of the cottages are 18th century and of brown heathstone or grey Purbeck stone or, as in the picture, a mixture of both.

ABOVE: **SUTTON POYNTZ**

Devoted readers of Thomas Hardy will know Sutton Poyntz as the Overcombe of *The Trumpet Major*. The mill worked by Hardy's miller William Loveday is no longer in use but the "large, smooth millpond" to the north survives as a beauty spot. So, of course, do the hills to the north of the village and their fine views of Weymouth and Portland, the latter likened by Hardy to "a great crouching animal tethered to the mainland". On one hillside is the figure of George III and his mount, cut into the chalk in 1807 in gratitude for his patronage of Weymouth.

ABOVE: WHITCOMBE

An 18th century brick wall encloses Whitcombe church, where Dorset's dialect poet Parson William Barnes began his ministry in 1847 and took his last service in 1885. As a curate he interrupted one sermon here to announce that nearby hayricks were ablaze, then joined his flock in the firefighting. The church stands on a pre-Conquest site and contains two fragments of Saxon crosses and some medieval wall paintings, one of which depicts St Christopher. The nave is part 12th century and part 18th and the tower carries the date 1596. The building, whose dedication has been lost, is now cared for by the Redundant Churches Fund.

OPPOSITE: WEST STAFFORD

West Stafford is Thomas Hardy's Froom-Everard and provides the setting for his short story *The Waiting Supper*. It is a village of the Frome, standing near the point where this river meets its tributary the South Winterborne. Thatched roofs are plentiful not only on cottages but the Wise Man pub, an old barn converted for bed and breakfast and even the bus shelter. Stafford House dates from 1633 and St Andrew's Church, tightly hemmed in by the highway and houses old and new, was rebuilt in 1640, though the tower may be earlier.

ABOVE: LOWER BOCKHAMPTON

Few villages anywhere have stronger literary connections than Higher and Lower Bockhampton, for it was at the former that Thomas Hardy breathed his first breath and took his first steps and at the latter that he began his formal education. Hardy was born in 1840 in a cottage built by his great-grandfather and occupied by the family from 1801. In 1848 he started school in the building pictured left before transferring to another school at Dorchester the following year.

OPPOSITE: LOWER BOCKHAMPTON

The River Frome and cottages at Lower Bockhampton, renamed Mellstock by Hardy. Surviving buildings include the original keeper's cottage in Yellowham Wood, described in *Under the Greenwood Tree*. Both this novel and *Far from the Madding Crowd* were written in the thatched cob cottage at Higher Bockhampton where Hardy was born. The cottage is now a National Trust property.

ABOVE: **PUDDLETOWN**

A terrace of Victorian cottages, strikingly built in Portland stone, presents an unusual frontage to travellers passing along the A35 at Puddletown. This part of the village was substantially redeveloped in the 19th century, thanks largely to squire John Brymer, of Ilsington House. He is the man behind the village's Victorian terraces, which Newman and Pevsner describe as "fearsome"!

ABOVE: PUDDLETOWN

Somewhat less fearsome is the old Reading Room (right), built in 1870 and another product of the Brymer regime. "They were all designed, it seems, by a firm of land surveyors, Wainwright and Heard, of Shepton Mallet. One is not surprised to discover that," say Newman and Pevsner. But a detour beyond Puddletown's two main roads reveals that there is more to the place than might be imagined. It still boasts a square, a green and some attractive old cottages. It is also practically surrounded by houses of a grander description, including Ilsington, Athelhampton and Waterston Manor, which Hardy made the home of his heroine Bathsheba Everdene. Puddletown's original name was Piddle. Hardy, who had relatives living here, called it Weatherbury in *Far From the Madding Crowd*.

ABOVE: TOLPUDDLE

Tolpuddle is arguably the most famous village in England, thanks to six farm labourers whose efforts to feed their families earned them transportation to Australia in 1834. They were penalised for putting pressure on landowners after their wages were cut from ten shillings (50p) a week to seven (35p). More than 150 years later trade unionists still pay tribute to the Tolpuddle Martyrs by marching through the village once a year. The thatched shelter in the picture was erected on the centenary in 1934. Behind it (left) is the stump of the dying sycamore tree where the martyrs held their meetings.

ABOVE: PIDDLETRENTHIDE

Piddletrentide takes the first part of its name from the River Piddle and the remainder from its value in 1086, when it was assessed for the Domesday Book at 30 hides. The cottages are of various styles with flint as a dominant ingredient. Many are connected to the road by little bridges across the modest Piddle stream. The parish church is large and predominantly Norman; the Victorian school has gates that are 500 years old and come from Lady Margaret Beaufort's tomb in Westminster Abbey!

INDEX

THE VILLAGES OF DORSET

A DORSET BIBLIOGRAPHY

FURTHER READING

Ashley, Harry: *The Dorset Village Book* (Countryside, 1984); *Dorset, A Portrait in Colour* (Countryside, 1986); *Dorset Inns* (Countryside, 1987); *Dorset Yarns* (Countryside, 1988)

Benfield, Eric: *Purbeck Shop — A Stoneworker's Story of Stone* (Ensign, 1990)

Brett, Ernest: *Six Men on the Stour* (Guttridge and Topp, 1985)

Brown, Mary: *Dorset Customs, Curiosities and Country Lore* (Ensign, 1990)

Burnett, David and Julian Comrie: *Dorset, The County in Colour* (Dovecote, 1991)

Cecil, David: *Some Dorset Country Houses* (Dovecote, 1985)

Chilver, Kathleen M: *Holdenhurst, Mother of Bournemouth* (Bournemouth Local Studies, 1956, 1980)

Coker, John and Thomas Gerard: *Coker's Survey of Dorsetshire* (Wilcox 1732, Dorset Publishing 1980)

Cullingford, Cecil N: *A History of Dorset* (Phillimore, 1980)

Draper, Jo: *Dorset, The Complete Guide* (Dovecote 1986); *Thomas Hardy, A Life in Pictures* (Dovecote, 1989)

Edwards, Elizabeth: *A History of Bournemouth* (Phillimore, 1981)

Fair, John and Don Moxom: *Abbotsbury and the Swannery* (Dovecote, 1993)

Gant, Roland: *Dorset Villages* (Hale, 1985)

Gardiner, Dorothy: *Companion into Dorset* (Methuen, 1937)

Goldsworthy, Margaret: *The Dorset Bedside Anthology* (Arundel, 1951)

Good, Ronald: *The Lost Villages of Dorset* (Dovecote, 1987)

Guttridge, Roger: *Dorset Smugglers* (Dorset Publishing, 1984); *Dorset Murders* (Ensign 1990); *Ten Dorset Mysteries* (Ensign, 1989); *Blackmore Vale Camera* (Dovecote, 1991)

Guttridge, Roger, Roger Holman and Roger Lane: *The Landscapes of Dorset* (Ensign 1991)

Hardy, Thomas: *Far From the Madding Crowd* (1874); *The Return of the Native* (1878); *Tess of the d'Urbervilles* (1891)

Hutchings, Monica: *Dorset River* (Macdonald, 1956); *Inside Dorset* (Abbey Press, 1965)

Hutchins, John: *History of Dorset* (1774, 1796-1815, 1861-70)

Kelly's Directory of Dorsetshire 1931 (Kelly's, 1931)

Legg, Rodney: *Purbeck Island* (1989); *Cerne's Giant and Village Guide* (Dorset Publishing, 1986); *Exploring the Heartland of Purbeck* (Dorset Publishing, 1986); *Lulworth and Tyneham Revisited* (Dorset Publishing, 1985); *National Trust Dorset* (Dorset Publishing, 1987); *Purbeck's Heath* (Dorset Publishing, 1987); *Literary Dorset* (Dorset Publishing, 1990)

Mason, Ivan: *Pubs and the Past, Hostelry and History in Dorset* (Mason, 1992)

Mee, Arthur (ed): *Dorset* (Hodder & Stoughton, 1939); *Hampshire with the Isle of Wight* (Hodder & Stoughton, 1939)

Mills, A. D: *Dorset Place-Names, Their Origins and Meanings* (Ensign 1990)

National Trust, The: *Corfe Castle* (National Trust, 1988)

Newman, John and Nikolaus Pevsner: *The Buildings of England: Dorset* (Penguin, 1972)

Osborne, George: *Dorset Curiosities* (Dovecote, 1986)

Peters, John (ed: Roger Guttridge): *Bournemouth Then and Now, A Pictorial Past* (revised edition Ensign, 1990)

Pitfield, F. P: *Dorset Parish Churches A-D* (Dorset Publishing, 1981); *Purbeck Parish Churches* (Dorset Publishing, 1985); *Hardy's Wessex Locations* (Dorset Publishing, 1993)

Popham, David and Rita: *The Book of Bournemouth* (Barracuda, 1985)

Redundant Churches Fund: *Churches in Retirement, A Gazetteer* (HMSO, 1990)

Roscoe, Ernest (ed): *The Marn'll Book* (Blackmore, 1952)

Royal Commission on Historical Monuments: *Historical Monuments in the County of Dorset* (HMSO)

Treves, Sir Frederick: *Highways and Byways in Dorset* (Macmillan, 1906, 1935)

Wallis, A.J: *Dorset Bridges: A History and Guide* (Abbey Press, 1974)

Wansbrough, Richeldis: *The Tale of Milton Abbas* (Dorset Publishing, 1974)

Williams, C.L. Sinclair: *Puddletown, House, Street and Family* (Dorset Record Society, 1988)

THE LANDSCAPES OF

DORSET

WORDS BY

ROGER GUTTRIDGE

PHOTOGRAPHS BY

ROGER HOLMAN AND ROGER LANE

NEW PAPERBACK EDITION

The combined forces of nature and man have given Dorset a rich environmental heritage whose landscapes are many and varied. They range from the smooth shores of Poole and Bournemouth to the rugged cliffs of Purbeck, from the rich green pastures of the Stour Valley to the soft purples of Hardy's "blasted heath", from the lonely hills and vales of North, West and Central Dorset to the bricks and tiles of the south-east conurbation. They include many special features which people travel long distances to see — the unique Chesil Beach stretching eight miles from Abbotsbury to Portland, the man-made Cobb which has sheltered boats at Lyme for centuries, Lulworth's famous Cove formed by a near-perfect ring of rock encircling the bay, the south coast's highest sea-cliff at Golden Cap.

In *The Landscapes of Dorset*, photographers Roger Holman and Roger Lane have captured the many faces of Dorset by exploiting their intimate knowledge of the area. Some of their subjects are familiar, many are not, but in both cases the landscapes have been framed in an original manner. Subtleties of light and nuances of tone are used to maximum effect, creating an amazing series of images which capture the true glory of each chosen landscape.

Some of the images are drawn from the huge personal collection which the two photographers have built up over many years; others have been gathered specifically for this book. Each is accompanied by a concise and informative text by Dorset writer Roger Guttridge, whose words set each view in the context of its past and present and, where appropriate, its future. The result is a book whose visual power will inevitably enhance our awareness and appreciation of the landscapes of Dorset and, through this, perhaps improve the chances of their preservation for future generations.

PAPERBACK EDITION · 96 PAGES · MAP & INDEX
80 COLOUR PHOTOGRAPHS · £9.95

ALSO AVAILABLE FROM ENSIGN PUBLICATIONS

A CALENDAR AND A SERIES OF GREETINGS CARDS BASED ON *THE VILLAGES OF DORSET* ARE NOW AVAILABLE. A SERIES OF GREETINGS CARDS BASED ON *THE LANDSCAPES OF DORSET* IS ALSO AVAILABLE.

OTHER BOOKS BY ROGER GUTTRIDGE

TEN DORSET MYSTERIES £6.95

DORSET MURDERS £6.95

HERITAGE IN DORSET AND THE NEW FOREST £7.50

HAMPSHIRE MURDERS £6.95

COMING SOON

SMUGGLER'S WALKS IN DORSET £4.99

FOR DETAILS OF THESE OR ANY OF OUR OTHER BOOKS, CALENDARS OR CARDS CONTACT :-

ENSIGN PUBLICATIONS

2 REDCAR STREET

SOUTHAMPTON SO1 5LL

TEL 0703 — 702639

FAX 0703 — 785251